Cenotaph 1999

The Late Romances 1997

Apocrypha 1991

Heartwood 1988

For the New Year 1984

Cenotaph

Cenotaph

POEMS BY

Eric Pankey

NEW YORK

ALFRED A. KNOPF

2000

THIS IS A BORZOI BOOK
PUBLISHED BY ALFRED A. KNOPF

Library of Congress Cataloging-in-Publication Data
Pankey, Eric.
Cenotaph : poems / by Eric Pankey. — 1st ed.
p. cm.
ISBN 0-375-40764-2
I. Title.
PS3566.A575C46 2000
811'.54—dc21   99-31088
CIP

Manufactured in the United States of America
First Edition

For Harry Ford

In memory

Don't even hear the murmur of a prayer.
It's not dark yet, but it's getting there.

—Bob Dylan

Contents

Contents

Contents

Contents

Cenotaph

See That My Grave Is Swept Clean

Words are but an entrance, a door cut deep into cold clay.

I say, *A late sky flagged with jade; ice on the pear blossoms.*
I say, *A thrush of cinnabar in the lily's throat.*
Behind each assertion, each gambit, I could place a question
  mark.

Behind each question, a residue of longing, half-assuaged,
An argument of brine-edged light the moon, your stand-in,
  doles out,
Grain by grain. Behind each question, a hook blackened with
  rust.

Begin with a clay bank, a chill wind's insufflation.
Begin with thumbflint, a fever, some sticks to fire the kiln.
Are words but an entrance? *Words are but an entrance.*

ONE

The Kingdom of God Likened to a Deer Carcass

What the crow abandons, worms relish.

If I stare long enough at these remains
I will imagine a kingdom undone:

Surveyed. Staked off. Limestone and ivory.
A cathedral built upon a temple.

This bone a buttress. That one a crossbeam.
Every altar stone bloodless and sun-bleached.

Every chapel floor swept clean by the wind.
For now, wind shudders the collapsing ribs,

Swirls up a mote of fur like milkweed silk,
And touches the ruin intricately.

What the wind forsakes, dogs will drag away.

The Ephemera of August

I hung the heavy, beheaded body on the blade,
Flung it over the gate for the crows to reckon with.
The hoe that killed a snake could not dislodge a nettle.
The nettle, deep-rooted, had staked its claim.
                                              That summer
I was buried in water. The tired air burned my lungs,
Lifted my body—*the body*—the preacher held down.
I was buried in water and raised. Heaven was mine,
An heirloom bestowed, at the hot close of those Last Days.

August Heirloom

All this was almost mine,
I who own nothing
                    but debt,
But a vacancy that accrues,
That haunts each room like a ghost,
Like the memory of a ghost cast out.

All summer the cicada tooled the maple's copper air.
All summer the cicada sharpened its awl.

In the mirror's shallow
A single star holds on like a nail in the wall.
The sky's dark corner is scratched glass.

One more word.
One more word sapped of its meaning
Like an unconfirmed miracle,
Like the weightless bauble the cicada sloughed.

Lunar Ode

O spare charity and arctic ash,
O knuckle of bone spur and pox,

I live beneath your shipwrecked light
As one lives with a canker or a curse,

As a logician in a farce, rational
Even as the stick comes down with a slap.

What is love when your heart is a quarry,
A cipher of basalt, a drought's memory?

What are proverbs but petty sounds
From a cracked jaw and a parched throat?

Like the ox, you know the yoke and the switch.
Like the ox, you turn the millstone,

Arrive where you started, worse for wear.
Every word is a slip of the tongue:

Mute, sibilant, liquid, a dream of rain,
Rubbed-up static. You own what a penny will buy:

A dented thimble, a bushel of husks.
How much debt can one take on? How much doubt?

I live beneath your shipwrecked light
As one trapped beneath a flooded deck: panicked,

Breathless, unsure if I rise or if I fall.
O for even the moon's light, for an iota of air.

Keepsake

Not the seed pearl, but the juniper
Skewed by wind, baffled,
A vacant zigzag in the elaborate dusk,
A sable altar there on the headland,
That tonight grants calm.

Having lost its oar in the surf,
The wind rehearses a circle
Through the copse of partridge berry and spruce.
The heavens never thought to map
This world afloat in formaldehyde.

Called back. Called back.
The starlight reeks of tallow,
The tallow of flesh.

Dream Landscape with the Old Brickyard Road Creek and Blind Willie Johnson

I have returned to the creek, to the current-scalloped sand,
The mud bank that gives and gives against onrush and
 backwash,

To the gust-cobbled surface sun-flecked with amber, the sky
As bright as icemelt, or blue, in deep shade, or buttermilk,

At times, more depth than surface, black as charred fircones,
 or rain,
Rain at night and a slide guitar troubling an old hymn

That I have no voice to sing, but still discern from the hush
Of water oaks and willows, the full reservoir of wind,

The nighthawk and the field mouse, a voice calling from the
 porch,
And having returned to the creek, to these oxbow shallows,

I wait, hell-bent, as one waits for Judgment Day, knowing
With one or two steps, he can ford the depth and distance
 home.

The Wind's Reliquary

What rain does not flood, the wind defaces.
Let the briar and the bramble come up.

Let the thorn feed what can feed upon thorns.
The wind, the wind says, throwing its voice.

Let the briar and the bramble have dominion.
Let the briar and the bramble house the snake.

What is a body but the wind's disdain?
What is a temple but wind turned inside out?

The wind offers the groom a helix of leaves.
The wind enters like a locksmith.

The wind rattles the panes, stirs the gleanings,
Shudders canvas and rigging.

The wind withdraws like water into an aquifer,
A thousand years ago or a thousand more,

Then a stratum cracks and what will rise rises,
An antique trove (older than a cistern,

Older than a tongue of fire, than a votive vessel)
Scattered beyond reclamation.

Where gods are named, one at a time like newborns,
The wind mouths the words of a lullaby.

The Wind's Reliquary

In the Book of Secrets, the wind scrawls in the margins.
In the Book of Secrets, the wind underlines its name.

The wind falls belly-down in a culvert, hisses through the
cypress.
The wind bestows at random randomness.

The Crossroads

Is it for the enigma of the hour?
Is it for the headlight, the klieg light,
The moon's ephemera and jurisdiction,
The stutter of a film,
An hour stricken, scoured, but not struck
That I allow my shadow to be cast?

                                        O to be nothing
To You.
            Thou art a snuffed wick
In a tumbler of oil, a trickle of smoke,
Garish and at loose ends in the undivided dark.

The nettle bed whispers *psalm and lament,*
Psalm and lament expecting neither.
I cannot strike a match or find the fuse.
The harvest is the wind's gesture,
Torchlight on the gleanings,
A hollow cathedral of chaff at the crossroads.

TWO

Cold Spring Brook

1.

How does light affirm in its passing,
Moving as it does, like this water
Toward its diffuse, estuarial edge,
Running tidal through the wide green range
Of wetland shallows, rose, and reedbrakes,
Fresh to salt: a merge, a convergence?
Bound as he is to *because* and *therefore,*
To the iteration of desire,
No knell, no toll can stay the hour.
The dark comes on. If *no* is the dark,
Should not light in its passing affirm?
To live in time is to be keelhauled,
Dragged and dragged beyond a single breath.
But breathe he must, so he breathes in.

Cold Spring Brook

2.

He builds the entire composition
Around an error—a sable-hair brush,
Slipped from his hand, salted Chinese white
Across a deep wash of ultramarine—
An error he hides by accentuation:
On all sides a thunderstorm's cordon,
Cold Spring Brook overfull at high tide,
A rain-stung gust across the causeway,
A dust slurry that mars the window.
The margins of what he surveys bleed
Into one green, one gray, one darkness:
His own reflection mere silhouette—
Featureless, suspended there, then effaced
Within the lightning-quickened instant.

3.

He has made of the narrow threshold
Between *landscape* and *contemplation*
An unlit altar where he augurs,
Where the thicket reads as a pathway,
Dusk as the dross of molten metal,
As blown smoke, driftwood's mineral ash,
Where memory becomes desire
Without alchemy or revelation,
Without the sediment of regret.
How indivisible the thing he meant
To render. Under his heart's crucible,
What remains unsaid waits as tinder—
Jackstraw and light wood—that will not catch,
Doused as it is by the cold, damp breeze.

Cold Spring Brook

4.

One June, after weeks of no rain,
The beach-edge of the marsh caught fire:
Wind lit the tall grass, wick after wick.
The stalks flared to filaments, cracked,
And sowed sparks to the ragged sand ledge.
Then the wind turned and a halfhearted rain
Haggled with what remained of the blaze.
By summer's end what damage there was
Was overgrown, a tangle of wild rose
Extending its claim on the low dunes.
In the time in between, he watched
The wide sickle of char glisten in rain,
Then green, consumed, as it had been by fire,
By a restless, wild welter, redeemed.

5.

It began as a sketch, and remains such,
Six or eight lines of charcoal dragged
Across the paper's tooth: the jetty,
The clapboard studio, copse of rose,
The Sound a flat expanse, an island
Where the white sky and white water fade
Into a boundary of early fog.
By habit, he troubles the page,
Reworks and overworks the surface:
Saw grass and heather here, a cedar edged
In shade there, until all is darkness,
A moment of morning cast as nocturne.
For once, he leaves well-enough alone,
Leaves the world, in its abstraction, true.

6.

The crow lives in the aftermath,
The osprey in the precarious *now*.
He lives somewhere in between, mistakes
The wreckage of his sin for punishment.
He knows only the sleepwalker's way,
The cartography of dusks and half-light,
The dull current from Deep River down.
And when he follows a line of thought
To its end, he finds a question mark.
How many questions can he yet ask
The proper answer to which is silence?
He stands at a threshold and looks out:
Night is a shadow box, a grave of silt,
A hollow that fills and fills with what falls.

7.

Say all of it can be taken back.
That each deed or word that worked its damage
Can be revised, withdrawn, stricken,
Ripped from the stained fabric of the moment,
From having-been-said, from having-been-done;
Say that forgiveness is not the issue,
But reparation. And afterward,
Forgetfulness, amnesia, the past
Showing no mark of the erasure,
No palimpsest of the act, the error. . . .
This is the lullaby that lulls him,
And as he falls asleep, the lines go slack,
Then tangle, voices in a little fugue,
A net that traps him under the surface.

8.

Oh, he half-sings. *The book of moonlight*
Is not yet written, nor half begun . . .
Until the words seem almost his own.
What comfort a refrain when it returns—
The same words sung again, yet somehow changed.
He looks through his own reflection out
And calculates the distance between
The Old Saltworks Road and the horizon,
Between the horizon and all that curves
Away, unseen, and yet in its place.
What comfort a refrain when it returns.
He lets the window frame and arrange
The arranged world in which he is held.
Bound as he is, he lets the dark come on.

THREE

Sacred and Profane Love

If it is indeed more fitting
To say that the world is an illusion,

Does it matter if what I behold is a gold braid
Inlaid upon ebony, or the wind-tousled jackstraw

Of salt hay that edges the marrow of the mudflats?
Does it matter if the gift the cicada leaves behind—

Hollow, dawn-enkindled, paper-thin—
Is the hieroglyph: *to begin again,*

Or the embodiment of cold light's sealed and sepia pallor
Beneath the ice floes of Europa?

In Titian's "Sacred and Profane Love,"
One woman is unclothed, exposed, and naked,

And the other is wrapped, decked, and bejewelled.
Each the image of the image of an idea.

Not an illusion, but an illustration.
Sometimes I can feel my heart in my throat.

Sometimes I can swallow nothing I put in my mouth.
What is a heart that consumes and is consumed?

How to Sustain the Visionary Mode

Wherever possible, avoid predication: *the night sea, the dark river, this rain.*

As in a dream, where the door opens into a cedar grove, and the haze conjures a screen of sorts onto which an ill-spliced film is projected, and the words, poorly dubbed, seem mere trinkets in a magpie's nest, let each object be itself.

Objects a magpie might hoard.

:The blown dusk-smoke of flies above the sacrifice: The flames inlaid and lacquered: The horizon, a single graphite line on rice paper:

Revelation is and will remain the subject: "Behold, I come quickly: hold that fast which thou hast, that no man take thy crown."

The moment present and full: thyme-sweetened honey, a New World of Gold, quick with what made it.

Let distractedness be an isthmus connecting the day to day, dazed with the fume of poppies.

Let the daydream, dimmed by slow rain, slip like a shuttle through the loom's scaffolding.

Let the rain rain all day on the slate, a province of rain, gray as the stone no longer quarried in these hills, gray as the pigeons tucked in the eaves:

The rain, the dark river, this night sea.

The Muse's Admonition

Party lights in the distance waver and dim.
Still, the shape of the island is distinct

Beneath these winter constellations.
I can almost hear the music,

The laughter, the low whispered secrets,
The vesper breeze you listen for

From the marble steps of the palazzo.
How long will you turn the thimble over

And over between your fingertips
Wondering what some future might deduce

From this one artifact? This trinket? This grail?
How long will you listen to a dove's woodwind

Echo between the bridges and arcades,
Between the pediments and crenellations,

To the celebrations of the Mass
Beyond the intricate marble lacework,

To the counterpoint of morning: stalled, stranded,
Snared in its instant of revelation,

An instant when a second note sounds
And harmony resolves what words will not?

To place one word after another is to lie,
You believe, and words are all I have offered.

The Muse's Admonition

You discard each gift and turn away.
As I might imagine the Auroras

Of a cold winter night from this latitude
(A field of poppies, a realm where gold

Is the ferment of gold, a field of wheat
Swept by wind as the sun flares and goes out...)

You begin with nothing, and give nothing shape.
The world begins with a pomegranate seed,

With the bones of a bolus,
With an oar creaking in its lock,

With the open door of a cathedral
Where each taper and votive is snuffed.

A wren clatters against glass. A wren darts
Through vining smoke and lifts to the dark

Of the dome's *trompe l'oeil.* The world begins
As a world begins: with a knotted rag

Soaked in gasoline. With a single match.
With just enough wind to blow out the match.

What name can I give you in this moment
Of creation, this moment of regret?

What name can I give you that you might turn,
You who are not of the angels, but bear their pain:

The dragonfly fury of their pulse,
The endless distance of their jackal dreams,

The constant solder-burn of foreknowledge,
The lead coins they pocket to stay earthbound?

The world begins as dust, as flooded cobbles,
Planks thrown down crisscross across the square.

A wasp on the lip of a wineglass,
The air, as always, fragrant:

Almond, drizzle, the canal's high water.
An orange pricked with cloves. Nets hung up to dry.

I am yours as your shadow is yours,
And when I withdraw at noon, or loom

At sunset, distorted and torn by
The stone arabesques, that is my habit

And not an act of mischief or treachery.
What name can I give you that you might hear

And in hearing, turn, as if to your own voice
Spoken from the sheltered dark of here and now?

You close your eyes and all is swept
Like dust from a parapet.

You open your eyes and dust settles back.
The city is a maze and yet at each turn

The Muse's Admonition

I find you always looking outward, away,
Beyond the Lagoon's bollards and beacons,

And, as in a nightmare, trailing the one
Who in turn trails you, you cannot decide

To stop or retreat or move ahead.
The object of such a pursuit

Is your own heart and its affliction:
Furious, at odds with itself,

Yet unmoved. To burn not with desire,
But with your own purgation, is that love?

The world begins and fills with what divides:
Paper lanterns' sallow light,

Waves lifted and set down, threshed to foam.
The sky addled with stars. The sky empty.

A mouth opening in a seizure.
A mouth opening to speak.

The Pilgrim's Departure

Now that the sedge and reed warblers
Shuttle between rush and hedges

And the marsh harrier's shadow
Dredges the salt flats

And the moon drops like a coin into a poorbox;
Now that the green brackish air,

Jaspered with haze, is stained at the edges,
The dead ends, dark alcoves, and quays

Open to arcades and alleyways,
Canals and thoroughfares,

And the way before me seems a way
For once not overlooked but afforded.

Last night in this empty campo
One by one the children were called in

From their game of tag around the wellhead.
How long has it taken me to learn

That no two sins are the same
Except they be forgiven.

Touched and one is changed.
No words left but the words

I remember: one is *goodbye.*
The other is on the tip of my tongue.

From the Estate of Spent Magic

Far off, the cricket crouches in the rain,
Strikes and strikes flint against steel,

Yet nothing sparks. Nothing catches.
I breathe in the dulling and opiate extract

Of night air and breathe it out again.
How is one led back past borders

Cordoned by deception and blame?
How is one led back when what is left

Is a ragged splinter, a swarm at the heart?
When the resurrection is the mere disclosure

Of the risen and you have been left behind?
What I have renounced is here at hand:

Salt that ignites the flames to blossom,
A way with words, a charm or two.

My one remaining book is infested with moths:
Whole spells, equations, and proofs gnawed away.

Between its pages: torn wings, ghostly dust.
The sky before me is an open ledger

From which the numerals have been erased.
One by one, fireflies, little amphorae of light,

Flare then disappear, disappear then flare:
Light without heat, and like me, barely here.

The Storm's End

The tarpaulin of rain torn away
Revealed a mock moon, a placebo
That dissolved in the humid dusk, untouched.

I followed a shadowline's muzzy edge,
Tasted the air, an electuary of words:

Iodine sublimed to a violet vapor,
The rank sulfur of tidal mudflats,
Musk masked by honey and salt rose.

I followed the creek, silted wide and shallow,
Beyond its delta to the map-dark of shoals

And, in those shallows, knelt as one kneels
At the end of a long and solemn pilgrimage,
As much in exhaustion as in reverence.

Homecoming

In time, thunder unshackles the rain.
The tassels of pollen fall. Dust,

Not breath, becomes the spirit's habit,
A finery of grit that gathers.

The jay, a blue throb in the holly,
Will scold as it bolts. What exile

Would not love the evergreen for its thorns,
The bird for the objection its sustains?

Cenotaph

1.

In the shallow domain of light's fitful flare,
An aviary of silt and minutiae drifts:
Pinpoints of citron, lilac, and sulfur,

Chips of shell-pink, a medusa's plume and ruff,
Coral cleaved and sundered, its dust offcast,
A constellation untied from its mooring.

How close the splintered sun that bracelets my wrist.
I reach down through to the edge of my seeing,
Beyond the fan vaulting of bladder wrack,

Through eel grass, through fallow shadow realms,
But I cannot pull you back to the surface,
You who are the body of my confession,
The cold weight of water that unearths a grave.

Cenotaph

2.

How long did the crescent moon trawl in the wake?
How long before the wake itself collapsed?
Before *North* and *South* held the same compass point,

Marked the same unfathomable distance home?
The night above you is a capsized hull:
No air finds its way through the caulked seams.

Nothing can hold the body for long.
Burned by salt's caustic, ropes would frazzle
And a canvas shroud, rived and flayed,

Would let loose the dark matter of its cargo.
Thus I offer only provisional words:
Each a winding sheet of reef wind and whitewash,
Each a tattered disguise for the travesty.

3.

From a distilled essence of quartz and rose,
From a gramarye of psalms and waves,
From strewn stones and a hazel rod,

I have built this empty tomb for you.
Let its fretwork of shadows be your raiment.
Let thunder's phosphor light your way.

Grief is weightless and hard-shelled
Like a seed carried on an updraft,
A seed set down on hostile soil.

I have built this empty tomb for you,
Which the tide will bury and not exhume.
Sleep as silt sleeps in its dark fall and depth.
Sleep as silt sleeps in its dark fall and depth.

FOUR

A Narrative Poem

The story of a story is order over chaos.
What is not known, or not yet perceived, is made known.

I am the Alpha and the Omega, John writes near the close
Of his Apocalypse. And then the chapter ends *Amen.*

Drunk, asleep on the couch, my father mumbled long
    columns
Of numbers he could not make balance. The open ledger

On the table matched figure for figure his sober dream.
There was no miscalculation. The story they told was true.

If Omega *is less than or equal to one, the cosmos*
Expands forever. If Omega *exceeds one, the cosmos*

Holds enough mass to contract, to collapse in upon itself.
Amen we say in conclusion, meaning *verily, truly.*

What is not known, I tell myself in consolation, will be.
The story of a story is order over chaos.

Comes a Time

There comes a time when you no longer believe the night and its one alibi, believe the snowlight in the orchard, the ice at the heart of the onion, the fever kindled by hummingbirds, the wind bruised by an angel's fall. There comes a time when the name you have called yourself in hope and lamentation— *I*—that charred wick, that ruined column that once held up the world, that incision that never quite healed—*I*—seems a makeshift marker for this body that sustained you. Did you believe the struck match purged the air you breathed? Did you believe you were ever poor, hungry for something more than the little that filled you day to day? "*I*...," you start to answer, "*I*...," knowing there comes a time.

From the Book of Lamentations

We all have a story to tell. Mine begins
With the gift of a knife. With a road of sand.
With bees like haze above a field of thistle.

Light falls silverpoint on a parchment of straw.
Snow dusts the wings of a crow. Rude at its edges,
The season is the season-between-seasons.

I hear my father mumble through his dreams.
The hailstone placed on his tongue turns each curse to song.
No, we were never poor, my mother counters.

When she died I went through her closet and found
Five hatboxes, each stuffed with unopened bills.
My hands are stained with pollen, raw with quicklime.

There is green ice on the creek, a web's torn gauze
Across closed eyes. My sister opens the door
And a wolf enters. Hornets nest in the eaves.

A dead body, stuffed with limestone shards, still floats.
My father left my brother a heart of rain.
And the back of his hand. *Here, all this is yours:*

This cold heart of rain and the back of my hand.
Unless the stone melts or the tongue is cut clean,
A voice goes on singing its song of exile.

So long, he sang, in lamentation.
The gift of a knife is bad luck, but this blade,
Well-edged, sharp to the point, has been my fortune.

The Disquisition of a Gesture

I am no longer that orphan,
Fostered by the shade of a gesture,
By a mirror's chipped silver,
The haze and flint of jalousied light,
The air, tinny with heat.
Each match cupped in the hand
Burned to a stub of char.

Once, a sentence was a ladder
And each word a rung.
But wherever I climbed or descended
A blackboard of smoke stood:
Ash on slate, illegible.
My story nonetheless.

My father lights my mother's cigarette
And then his own. Their faces,
Lit from below, seen from below,
Gather and harbor shadow like death masks.

They each inhale and hold in the smoke.
If I could read the clock
I would count the hours.

Bygones

What is the past but everything:
The *not-there* between memory
And foreground, between suffering
And a moment's hardened amber?
Still, each word gives way to silence
And I must reinscribe this scrawl,
This impermanent graphite ghost
As signature on these torn scraps.
In the end I will be voiceless.
The earth that held me down will hold
Me once again, unforgiven,
Without a plea. Once, I listened
And heard far off the firebreak
Ignite with the song of crickets.
I heard a cold wind at loose ends
In the brambles and witch hazel.
I heard my brother say his prayers,
Not as rehearsed words enacted,
But with a child's solemnity.
I heard the snap of a dog's jaw,
The thud when the truck knocked it down.
I heard the refrain, *I ain't got
No home in this world anymore,*
Stuck as these lines stick in my mind,
But the rest of the song was lost:
Each unsaid word driven in edgewise,
A silence etched by burin and acid.

A Confessional Poem

The story would not resolve itself for the telling. It remained not clouded exactly, but dense—like amber—with its own color and hardness, a surface and depth that mimic each other: light enters and takes a long time leaving, caught up in the sepia, the golds, the pale yellow of the river willow's leaves, the fog having lifted, but still remnant: the odor that rises from the book as you open it, the dead language of fossils in a jag of limestone, the honey on the blade as it's scraped from the combs. The story, if he tried to tell it now, would move *away* from the causal, like all matter, dark and light, from the trauma of creation.

Nocturne and Morning Song

Soon enough silence will reign.
                              No need
To subtract one more word from the clamor.
I walked out onto the frozen river,
Watched the darkness between stars take its shape,
A scattering of dust to the edge of things.
My parents were still alive, but I knew
That soon enough they'd be part of that dust,
The cold distance between each mote and speck
And what I breathed would be full and emptied
Of their presence.
                              My dreams are a child's dreams.
I remember nothing but the waking.
Let the maple drop its keys to the wind.
Let the bluejay jimmy the morning's latch.
Let each secret I have kept keep me safe,
O God of Clamor. O God of Silence.

The Cold War

My mother nods off. A lit cigarette
Elegant between her long fingers.
The arm of the divan riddled with burns.

Lightning, out of sync, preens the maple.

What is the square root of *yesterday*?
How do I solve for the door ajar?
There's no end to it, my father would say.

My mother nods off. A lit cigarette
Elegant between her long fingers.
The burns like islands on an oily sea,

The obsolete map of an archipelago
Where the Bomb was tested year after year.
There's no end to it, my father would say

And ask me to warm up his drink.
The unknown, the variable we call *it*.
Upholstery smoulders more than it flames.

Lightning, out of sync, preens the maple.

FIVE

Elegiac Variations

for Larry Levis

1. Mood Indigo

Ahead of me the day ahead

As I come down out of the Blue Mountain
Pine ridge dogwood
       a palimpsest of haze
A gully of cornflowers

Where is the pleasure of arrival
Now that *then* has become *now*

All that remains of the western night

Is the coal and indigo
       of a hawk's eyes
Coal and indigo and a grain of salt

And of the fog
     one drop on each thorn

How far I have come to be only here

Elegiac Variations

2. The Starling's Lullaby

Another day kindled and put out

Thus the crimped thread of smoke
Thus the ember motes that glint and fall

Thus the acrid aftertaste on my tongue

                               after so few words

The cedar's charred wand
The nettle bed's sloughed ash
The saltlight flint-gray on the marsh

It is hard to extinguish desire

All evening the starlings taunt
From the conflagration of the firethorn

What it burns it fuels with the soul

3. The Parable of the Vineyard

The moon
             its mouth sealed shut with wax
Maintains its vow of silence

Across a rain-washed range
Across the stripped vineyard
Across the blade of a pruning hook

Left to rust in a furrow
             you follow your father home

How can one not mistake
Intensity for purity
Paradise for these ill-lit shambles

By now the dark fields are wild with rose
And the thistle worn to a crown

Elegiac Variations

4. Three Crows

Three crows overthrow the canopy
And caw down in judgment

Still I count the streaks on the tulip

Cast the sun out of rust and haze

Compose and shape the landscape
By implication
                    fog on the creek
Shadow on the berry canes

Yes I have counted the crows
A trinity high in the pine

I was called but did not follow

I was called by name and did not follow

5. The Blues

How heavy the mortal body of Christ
Two angels hold half in the tomb
                              half out
On display for our pity
                    and for pity's sake

His face unrestored
                a bluish blur and canvas weave

No pain no suffering to be read
As compensation as consolation for our own

Lord I just can't keep from crying sometimes
Lord I just can't keep from crying sometimes
When my heart's full of sorrow
When my eyes are filled with tears
Lord I just can't keep from crying sometimes

6. Study for Rain

Between cypress and olive
                        the shadow of rain
The rag ends of rain blown clear
It rained and the rain stopped
How few of our certainties
                        resemble the truth

Rushlight cloudlight a dull smoulder
The hive a cask of untuned static
A tinderbox of sparks

Between the cypress and olive
                        the footpath winds
Where the marble's worn water pools

Had God not made pale honey
I should have said this rain was sweeter

7. Nocturne and Refrain

Now you may have the final word

As the salt creek overflows with tide
As the cutbank's grasses drift heavy
Like a dragnet in the flooded marsh
As a heron lifts from the surface
Without noise without proclamation
Emblem of itself
                  Swallows wheel
Wheels within wheels over the wetland
A rope goes slack a rope is pulled taut
And below an anchor scuffs the silt

Now you may have the final word

8. Confronting the Oracle in Fiesole

Only a lizard to show the way

Little green flame through the ruins
A wordless scrawl and scuttle on the Etruscan wall

Only a lizard to find a foothold of shade

If from the earth we come
If to the earth we return
Then there is in the end
                    no digression
The one way home is the one way home

Green and quicksilver in the sepia shadows
Green and quicksilver
                    the lizard holds still for now

For now still it holds its tongue

SIX

The Metaphysician's Insomnia

The wind kicks up surf and keeps him awake,
Whistling its plaint against the nailed-shut frame.
The ocean, in its phases, swells and shrinks.

He tries to remember the words to songs,
Building outward from their refrains. He counts
Backward from four hundred and sixty-eight,

But gives up, at last, before zero or sleep.
Daylight dismantles a scaffold of fogs,
Censors the seductive postures of stars.

He cannot bridge the threshold between sheer
Exhaustion and the dead-man's-float of dreams.
The ache of his aching body is so real

He understands, at last, what ecstasy means.
As always, a hairline crack separates
The noumenal from the phenomenal,

Sleep from waking, the poem from the fragment,
And yet it seems to him an ice-cut gorge,
A comet's wake, a fissure between meaning's

Irresolution and desire's closure.
He starts to recite "Stars of Tallapoosa,"
The meter allowing for plausible errors,

But the poem's final line vanishes like sugar
On his tongue: at first sweet, then a burn,
Then the bad aftertaste of a long night.

Divination at Chapman Beach

I mention the light on Cold Spring Brook,
—Where at the bend it abides, the tide gone slack—

Dull as a drop of solder on a teapot
Or, as fog lifted, clear as the fine grit

Of sandstone, raw sienna, and native umber,
And the light changes (or so I'll remember)—

Jade, a transparency of shadows,
Quicksilver at the edges, lampblack below—

And my hapless shorthand cannot keep up.
Thus, the teapot engenders a teacup,

And I read the configuration of leaves,
But seeing no sign of what I might believe,

Rinse it out in the sink. How the world began
I couldn't say, but no one was looking on.

What I mean to say has to do with the light,
How, though divided from the dark, it shifts

Mote by mote to the weight of its absence—
Unstable, volatile, a confluence—

Never seen, not even for a minute
As *itself*—a glint, a glister—wholly split

(A clock stopped at noontide, a gold nimbus,
A glare's unpied, undappled transplendence)

Divination at Chapman Beach

From the gloam of velvet, cross-hatch of charcoal,
Muddy wash, surface oil drawn to marble.

If the world were to begin at this moment,
Here, where the freshwater brook runs to salt,

God would behold a flat *S* of gray,
Not dovetail or pewter, but of the bank's own clay.

Then more blue than gray, like a nick in pewter,
Like a dove's blurred flight. Then a blue like water.

From the Sketchbook of the Demiurge

As one season stains the next,
All the world that was once *a* world
Bleeds through, muddies certainty,

Yet the windform of the pine—
Stunted, twisted, leeward-sharpened—
Can be cut out as a paper triangle,

Glued to a stick and recognized
As *pine*, as *the* pine, as *that* pine.
At center stage, a trapdoor waits

Through which the damned disappear
And he reads the hole as *hell*.
Or if a God, in a golden sun mask,

Rises, the aria low thunder
Given voice, a human voice amplified
Through a mask's crafted mouth-cone,

He reads the trapdoor as the cloud-rough surf
Of the firmament, and that harnessed body,
Hoisted up, as weightless and omnipotent.

He wakes each morning to a book of words,
To the handiwork of another.
He wakes and tries to make it all match up:

The bleached oar with the equinox.
The jellyfish with mica and plume.
The dove's call with a dragnet's pull.

From the Sketchbook of the Demiurge

The pine's whittled edge with an icon's stare.
The object and the word for the object,
As *object,* multiplied as if placed

Between two mirrors: infinite,
Clear to the limits of his seeing,
Yet as close as the glass's width.

He writes: *a resinous wick, a lampblack shadow,*
A riddle of wind, a storm tassel,
Then, with three ragged lines, draws a triangle,

Taking comfort you'll know what he means.

Winter in Revision

The holly, like a vessel of magic,
Lets loose a flock of cedar waxwings

(A bird not named for its flight or song,
But for its wingtip markings—*blunt sticks*

Of scarlet sealing wax). Green burns strong,
A barbed flame on a resinous wick.

If I could remember a morning
Not spurred by the cold of winter stars. . . .

Yet my days are spurred by winter stars.
Those that fall grow colder in falling.

The holly, like a vessel of magic,
Lets loose a flock of cedar waxwings.

How far I've fallen in my falling,
Pulled down by a ballast of secrets.

I do not remember flight or song,
But hard berries like blood in their beaks.

Prospero Considers the Last Days

What is love in his brackish blood
But pure air, an embolism,
A morning star rising amid
A dull miscellany of glare?
Though now he practices craft,
He still remembers enchantment.
He pours a drop of mercury
On a saucer and with a knife
Divides and divides the metal.
Waits and lets it recongregate:
Molten, yet cool to the touch. Poison.
He had imagined his love more like that.

The Unstrung Lyre

These unaccompanied words, *a cappella,*
May as well be words in an empty chapel:

Fire-gutted, cellar-cold, shadows gathered
In the pews instead of parishioners.

Are such words, spoken to no one, prayer?
The restless gibber of the heart,

Frantic, willing to say anything,
To beg mercy of what might silence it?

As bright as an Annunciation lily,
As a bowstring shimmering to stillness,

The Word is what I heard and cannot replicate.
This unstrung frame may as well be a loom

Upon which no tomorrow is woven,
Upon which no tomorrow is postponed.

Prospero in Purgatory

Wind riffles the marsh from sodden salt hay
To kingfisher green, from lead to gold ether,
From shale to slate to amethyst and pearl.

Long ago he gave up explicating the changes.
The footnotes grew longer than the text:
Digressions hemmed by qualification,

Observations overwrought with afterthought.
A recording secretary, he keeps the minutes—
The narrow shoal of fog and first light,

The drag of black drizzle across the dunes,
The shingle of rocks reflected in the delft—
In a crabbed shorthand of his own making.

Sometimes he nods off and misses a gust.
Sometimes he gives in to sleep and as he sleeps
Satan raises up a straw-built citadel,

Reigns for a millennium and is toppled.
Sometimes he wakes to a light so white
It seems the whole world has calcified.

What he sees he sets down as if the truth.

To the Magpie on the Roof of the Manger

You hid each star but one in a shallow shadow box,
A relic-filled cabinet of curiosities,

And let the wind rifle the tinder. And let the wind
Refurbish the straw, the stalls, and the dovecote's niches.

What happens to a moment held captive, a moment
Torn away, ransacked from the dull continuum?

In your beak, you hold a marble in which the world—
Shrunken, drawn long, upside down—is as round as the
     world

That deceives us with horizons and vanishing points,
The parallel rows of grapes that touch in the distance,

The *far away* where all is drawn together at last.
From here, I can even see myself in the marble—

Bent, distorted, the sky below me like a blue pit
Over which I hang headfirst, confused like the damned.

SEVEN

Without You

The water yields no distance to the oar.
Worn like a salt lick, the moon is consumed
At last. It gives up what it has to give.

Who will snuff the lamp swollen with glare?
Who will lift a fever's muslin and exhume
The thousand and one stories of my love?

The touch of your tongue was a voyage of wind-swells,
A swan's blurred and exquisite agitation,
Bloom on a briar, rain and wine on my lips.

Without you, hoarfrost silences the bells,
The low rafters of the Resurrection,
Not yet restored, molder behind canvas tarps.

Without you, the orchard is strewn with windfall.
Four walls and one burnt match are my hell.

Sandy Point Road: An Eclogue

Again the day begins: the hour like Galilee,
Both an instant in time and a map's coordinates

In which and on which I put faith. Three yellow jackets
Halo a glass of Jack Daniel's left out overnight.

The horizon—silvered, chalk-edged, figmental, level,
Depthless—attenuates the moment and fools the eye:

A thin repertoire of contrivances, a premise
Of edges, a line's repose between two blue-gray slabs.

Abstractus: dragged away. To abstract the landscape,
To be in it in exile. Again the day begins.

There is a path before me and I follow it. *Home?*
Yes, there is a path before me and I follow it.

Landscape and Self-Portrait

Two notes and an interval of silence. *Not here*
It seems to say, calling attention to itself.

If it is true that truth is ever new, as now,
Then the mockingbird's eye is the vanishing point.

These lines, which will never intersect, appear to.
How easily we are fooled. That dull red palm-print

On the cave wall is not blood but iron oxide.
A hand. Not a heart. The pigment, of earth itself,

Held fast and holds. The image was the image at hand.

Studio with Vanitas *Still Life*

The body, a vessel of shadow,
Seems more when pricked and in pain.

A broadside of light divides the dark,
A flash followed by thunder, then rain.

And the soul would weigh nothing at all
If not for the scruple of its stain.

A broadside of light divides the dark,
A flash followed by thunder, then rain.

Still, the skull, snuffed candle, and rank fruit
Comfort like the words of a refrain.

Dividing the dark, a broadside of light,
A flash followed by thunder, by rain.

Underdrawing

The wind-brindled marsh surface,
The dunes overthrown by flood tide,
The length of Salt Island Road to its dead end,

Are now a charcoal stain burnt beneath zinc and titanium,
The abandoned gestures of a night's edge.
Nonetheless, a fish hawk hunkers beneath the downpour:

A smudge beyond the blown rain, a ragged effigy
Of nothing I can honestly name. Yet in my idleness,
I ravel the hermeneutics of talon and wingspan,

Of updrafts, wind shear, and angles of descent.
I wipe the glass, but it fogs again. I wipe the glass,
But soon cannot see through the marks my hand has left.

Words to a Ghost

I put my hand on my heart, but pledge nothing.
My word is a lodestone of gravity

That tastes of copper on the tongue,
A slurry that will not hold.

I live with your bequest
As one lives with a broken rib,

That ember of ache, ash-banked and cold,
That sliver of ice the whiskey consumes.

You may ask my forgiveness one more time.
You may ask my forgiveness one more time

But first you must breathe.

The Anniversary

1.

The constellation Virgo harbors a black hole at its center, but tonight I see the moon, ordained, a basilica of salt, mouthing its one secret like a saw-whet owl, and all that might be culled, collected, and classified beneath it, named as a disposition of objects, as a taxonomy, an order, a genus, or subject matter, is smeared with this salvaged and chalk-dry light, this fine-grained and corrosive distillate, this heirloom dust that gathers on the pearl button of the glove, its little satin noose.

The Anniversary

2.

When I said, "But tonight I see the moon," I did not tell the whole truth, for I have not even looked outside, but have relied on the conventions of memory, and with a word or two the moon, like a body under siege, wears thin outside my window, the moon forages in the attic, the moon is hauled up like a broken whetstone from a well, for that is what I do with a word or two: avoid scrutiny, avoid measuring the lead weight of my own heart.

Meditation at Hinkson Creek: Thanksgiving, 1980

The wolf knows nothing of the path I follow.
No trail of blood mars the snow or frozen scrim.

There is no lair, only ill-memory
Where one thought after another gutters

Like the sooty flame of a kerosene lantern.
Shadows stammer and loom, swell and retreat,

But no one clear note sounds amid the clamor.
Each word is but the mire of rumor,

The windblown parchment of a wasps' nest,
A ragged turban grafted to a branch,

Mindless as winter and without redress.
Somewhere the zero of night is struck

Like a match, like a steel spike with a sledge.
Somewhere the wolf tears at a throat,

At sinew, unhews its prey bone by bone
With care, with precision, but not devotion.

Somewhere my accuser waits as I wait.
Why have I made a god of my dull sins?

Between a feast and a prayer, the cold's lacuna,
Enough snow to erase the horizon,

To make the trail I came in on no more mine
Than the miserly wind's thin tithing,

Than the flooded creek's debacle of ice.

ACKNOWLEDGMENTS

The author gratefully acknowledges the editors of the following publications where these poems, many in earlier versions, first appeared: *American Literary Review:* "Lunar Ode"; *Bellingham Review:* "Sacred and Profane Love"; *Boulevard:* "The Wind's Reliquary"; *Cimarron Review:* "Divination at Chapman Beach"; *Colorado Review:* "Elegiac Variations 7"; *Crazyhorse:* "Cold Spring Brook"; *Delmar:* "Homecoming"; *Gettysburg Review:* "Dream Landscape with the Old Brickyard Road Creek and Blind Willie Johnson," "A Narrative Poem"; *Image:* "Elegiac Variations 4," "Landscape and Self-Portrait," "Studio with *Vanitas* Still Life"; *Iowa Review:* "Comes a Time," "A Confessional Poem," "Elegiac Variations 1,2,3,5,6,8," "How to Sustain the Visionary Mode"; *The Metropolitan Review:* "August Heirloom," "From the Sketchbook of the Demiurge"; *The Missouri Review:* "The Anniversary," "Bygones," "Cenotaph," "The Cold War," "To the Magpie on the Roof of the Manger," "Underdrawing"; *Natural Bridge:* "From the Book of Lamentations," "Words to a Ghost"; *The New England Review:* "From the Estate of Spent Magic," "See That My Grave Is Swept Clean," "The Unstrung Lyre"; *Re: Generations:* "Meditation at Hinkson Creek: Thanksgiving, 1980"; *Shenandoah:* "Prospero in Purgatory"; *Verse:* "Winter in Revision"; *The Wallace Stevens Journal:* "The Metaphysician's Insomnia"; *Witness:* "The Pilgrim's Departure"; *The Yale Review:* "Sandy Point Road: An Eclogue."

PERMISSIONS ACKNOWLEDGMENTS
AND OTHER TEXT SOURCES

Grateful acknowledgment is made to the following for permission to
reprint previously published material:

Special Rider Music: Excerpt from "Not Dark Yet" by Bob Dylan.
Copyright © 1997 by Special Rider Music. All rights reserved. Interna-
tional copyright secured. Reprinted by permission of Special Rider
Music.

Some of the poems from this collection borrow language directly from
external sources:

"The Blues (Elegiac Variations)," stanza 5: Excerpt from "Lord I
Just Can't Keep From Crying" by Willie Johnson. Used by permission.
Copyright Alpha Music Inc. Reprinted by permission of Alpha Music.

"From the Estate of Spent Magic," stanzas 5 and 6: Excerpts from
"Treatise on the Resurrection," in *The Nag Hammadi Library* (New
York: HarperCollins).

"How to Sustain the Visionary Mode," stanza 5: from Revela-
tion 3:11.

"A Narrative Poem," stanzas 2, 5, and 6: Excerpts from *Empire of
Light: A History of Discovery in Science and Art* by Sidney Perkowitz.
Copyright © 1996 by Sidney Perkowitz. Reprinted by permission of
Henry Holt and Company, LLC.

"Sacred and Profane Love," stanza 1: Excerpt from "Treatise on
the Resurrection," in *The Nag Hammadi Library* (New York: Harper-
Collins).

"See That My Grave Is Swept Clean," line 2: Excerpt from "For
the Examination of Ho-nan-fu: Song of the Twelve Months (with Inter-
calary Month)" by Li Ho, translated by Burton Watson, in *Chinese
Lyricism* (New York: Columbia University Press).

"Winter in Revision," lines 4 and 5: Excerpt from *Pedigree: The
Origin of Words from Nature* by Stephen Potter and Laurens Sargent
(New York: Taplinger Publishing). *Winter in Revision* is the title of a
collage by artist Debora Greger.

A NOTE ABOUT THE AUTHOR

Eric Pankey was born in Kansas City, Missouri, in 1959 and received his B.A. from the University of Missouri at Columbia and his M.F.A. from the University of Iowa. His first collection of poems, *For the New Year*, was selected as the winner of the Walt Whitman Award from the Academy of American Poets and published by Atheneum in 1984. In 1988, Atheneum published his second collection, *Heartwood*, which was reissued by Orchises Press in 1998. His next two collections were published by Alfred A. Knopf: *Apocrypha* in 1991 and *The Late Romances* in 1997. His work has been supported by fellowships from the National Endowment for the Arts and the Ingram Merrill Foundation. He is professor of English at George Mason University and teaches in the Master of Fine Arts Program. He lives in Fairfax, Virginia, with his wife, the poet Jennifer Atkinson, and their daughter, Clare Atkinson-Pankey.

A NOTE ON THE TYPE

This book was set in a typeface called Walbaum. The original cutting of this face was made by Justus Erich Walbaum (1768–1839) in Weimar in 1810. The type was revived by the Monotype Corporation in 1934. Young Walbaum began his artistic career as an apprentice to a maker of cookie molds. How he managed to leave this field and become a successful punch cutter remains a mystery. Although the type that bears his name may be classified as modern, numerous slight irregularities in its cut give this face its humane manner.

Printed by The Stinehour Press, Lunenburg, Vermont
Bound by Quebecor Printing, Brattleboro, Vermont
Design and composition by Robert C. Olsson